My name is HEART

Indranil Gupta, MD

Written by a Board Certified Pediatrician in the USA, Dr. G

MY BODY SERIES

Archway Publishing books may be ordered through booksellers or by contacting:

Archway Publishing
1663 Liberty Drive
Bloomington, IN 47403
www.archwaypublishing.com
844-669-3957

ISBN: 978-1-6657-0065-8 (sc)
ISBN: 978-1-6657-0063-4 (hc)
ISBN: 978-1-6657-0064-1 (e)

Print information available on the last page.

Archway Publishing rev. date: 04/14/2021

''Dedicated to our parents and teachers who refine us after our creation'' – Dr. G (Board Certified Pediatrician in the U.S.A.)

The heart and its neighbors

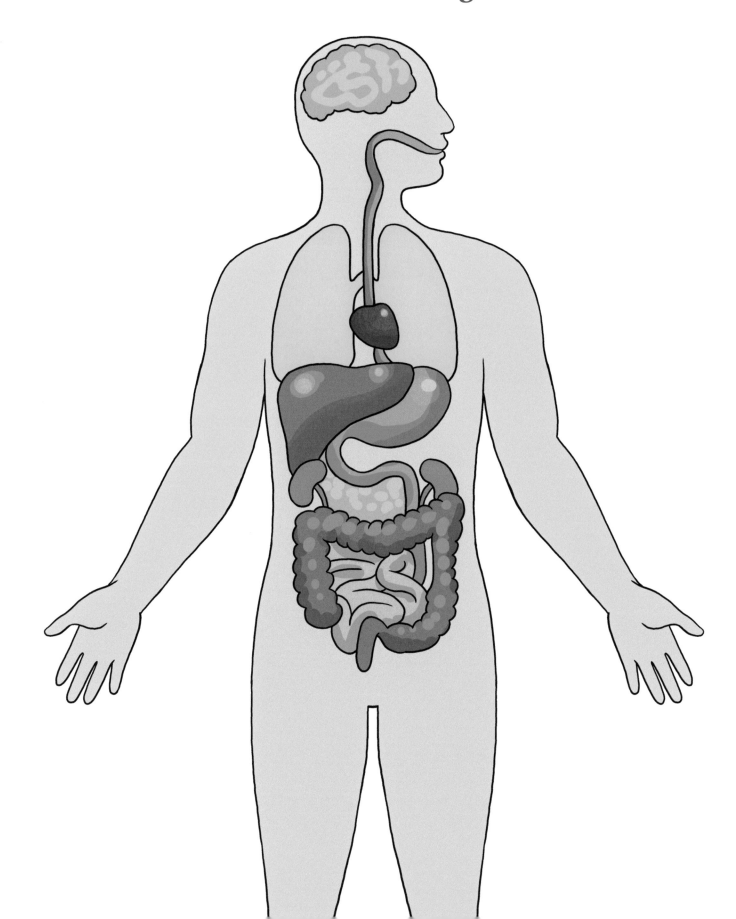

Goal of this book:

To help children learn about the heart and how to keep it healthy

Quotations:

"Knowledge is power" - Francis Bacon, 1597 (English Philosopher)

The old way of listening to the chest

The word 'Heart' originates from:

Greek: Kardia | Latin: Cordum | German: Herz

Who was the first open heart surgeon in the world?

Daniel Hale Williams.

He was the son of a barber.

He founded the first black-owned hospital in America.

He performed the world's first successful heart

surgery in the year 1893, in Chicago.

Who was the world's first heart transplant surgeon?

Christian Barnard.

He performed the world's first human to human heart

transplant on December 1967 in Cape Town, South Africa.

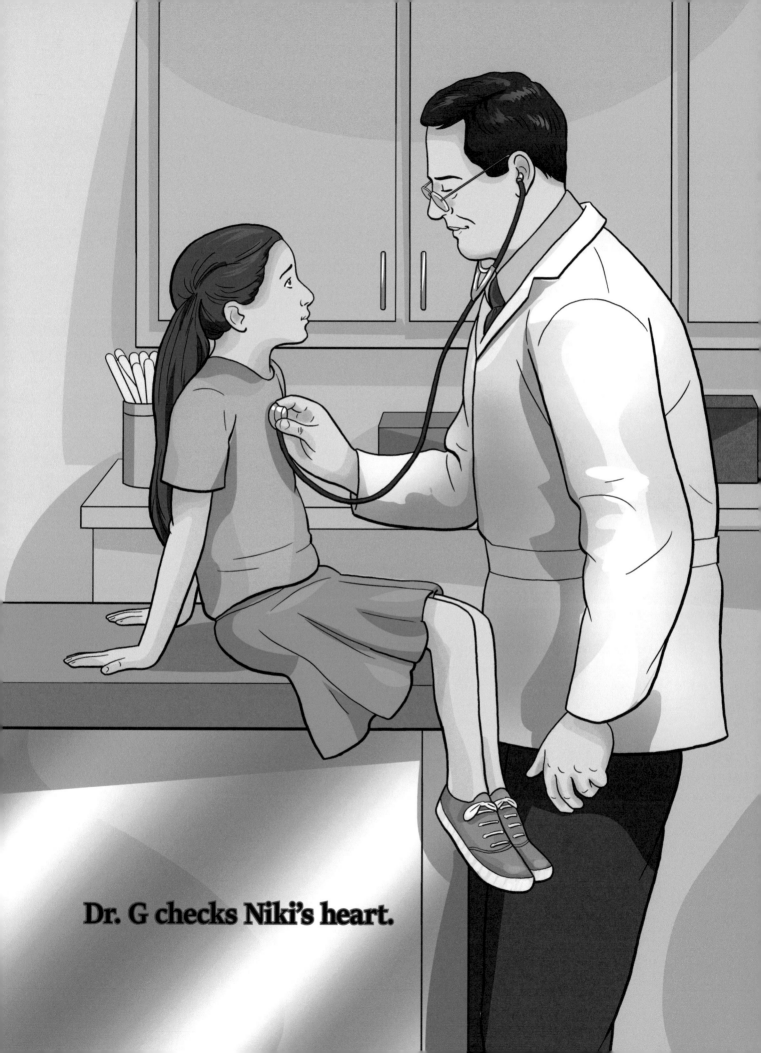

Dr. G checks Niki's heart.

Where do I live?

I live in your chest, right at the center

I hide behind your ribs, as they are my shelter

Lungs by my side are my close friends

We always work together, it never ends

If you listen close, you can hear my voice

"Pump-pump, pump-pump" is my noise

I am comfy in your chest, the place I call home

My name is Heart and I never feel alone

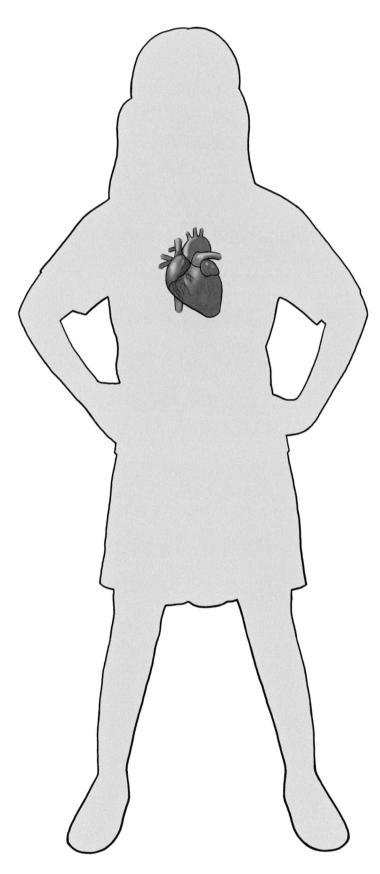

There's the heart!

What do I do?

I am always working, even when you sneeze

This is something that I guarantee

I talk to your brain and we work together

Pumping blood to make you feel better

I also send oxygen all around

To make sure your body is safe and sound

I never rest, never forget to beat

My name is Heart and together we're complete

Exercise makes Alex happy!

What makes me happy?

I feel so happy when we exercise

Let's get some fresh air and play outside

It's also important to drink lots of water

Staying hydrated makes us stronger

Don't forget to get enough sleep

If we wanna have fun, we need energy

All of these suggestions, you must remember

My name is Heart and we'll be happy together

What makes me sad?

I feel so sad when we're lazy

Laying around drives me crazy

Please be sure to eat healthy food

Fruits and veggies put us in a good mood

Playing video games can be a distraction

Instead, I like to get up and take action

Last but not least, please put the phone away

My name is Heart, let's have some fun today!

Alex looks so strong!

What keeps me going?

A healthy diet keeps me going

Eat right and we'll keep growing

Apple, orange, strawberry and cherry

I just know they'll make us merry

Broccoli, spinach and lettuce too

Must eat our greens, yes it's true

Fish and chicken are the way to go

My name is Heart and now you know!

Niki needs to recharge.

What slows me down?

Eating unhealthy slows me down

Too much sugar makes me frown

Fruit juice? Well, that's a no

But to fresh fruit, I say hello

Watch out for chicken nuggets and fries

Not so healthy, let's think twice

Junky snacks? I'd rather not

My name is Heart and that's all I've got!

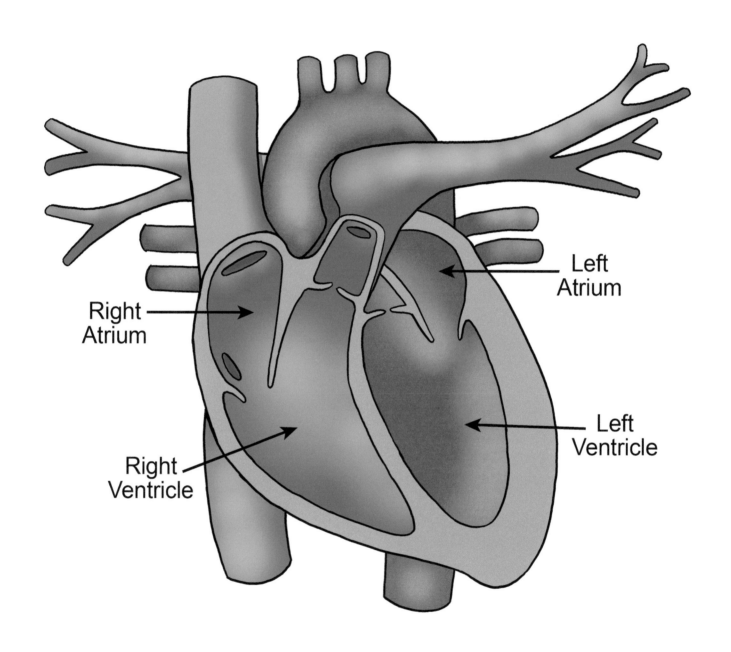

Right
Atrium

Left
Atrium

Right
Ventricle

Left
Ventricle

Real Heart

Do you know facts about the heart?

The heart has 2 atriums and 2 ventricles.

The heart beats 100,000 times per day, every day.

The heart pumps 2,000 gallons of blood every day.

The heart weighs as much as a ketchup bottle.

Your heart is about the same size as your fist.

Oxygen and nutrients are sent through the blood.

Newborn babies have the fastest heart rates.

On average, athletes have slower heart rates.

Electrocardiograms (ECG) check the heart's health.

A cardiologist is a doctor of the heart.

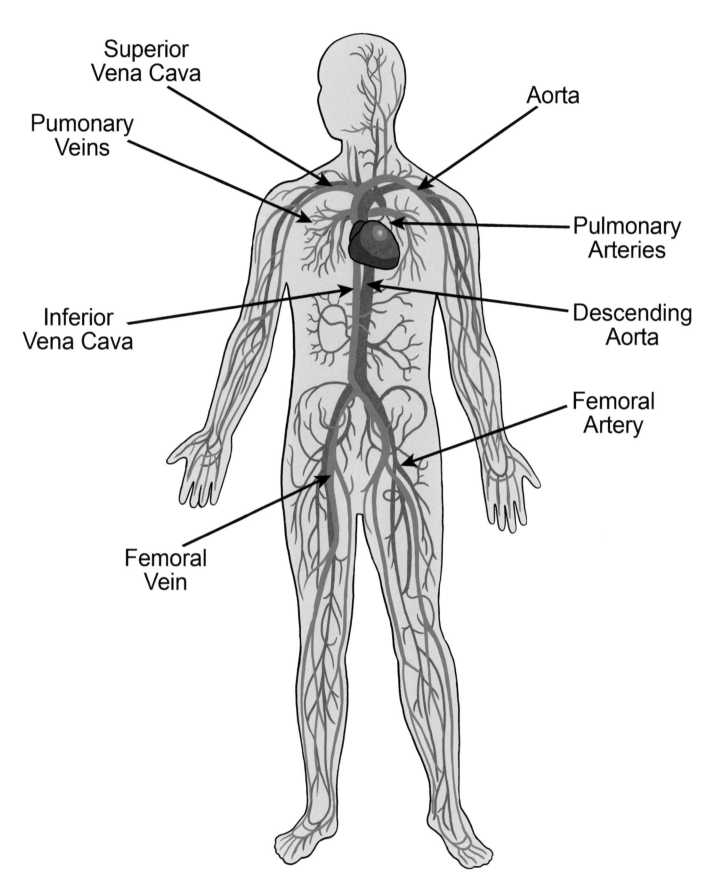

Superior
Vena Cava

Pumonary
Veins

Inferior
Vena Cava

Femoral
Vein

Aorta

Pulmonary
Arteries

Descending
Aorta

Femoral
Artery

Circulatory System

Do you know facts about heart disease?

1 in 100 children has a heart problem.

Heart disease prevents the heart from doing its job.

Common signs and symptoms of pediatric heart disease include:

· Chest pain
· Weakness
· Palpitations
· Stunted growth

· Difficulty breathing
· Dizziness
· Paleness
· Fatigue

If you see any signs and symptoms that are
concerning – you must see a doctor.

Fun Fact Questions

(1.) Where is the heart located?

Clue – *what part of the chest?*

(2.) How can you show the size of your heart?

Clue – *think of boxing*

(3.) Which animal has the biggest heart?

Clue – *think of the largest ocean creature*

(4.) Which creature has the smallest heart?

Clue – *a tiny creature that likes fruits*

(5.) Which land animal has the largest heart?

Clue – *a tall, long-necked animal in Africa*

(6.) Which creature has more than one heart?

Clue – *a sea creature with eight arms*

(7.) Before the invention of the stethoscope, how did doctors and nurses listen to the heart?

Clue – *no instrument was used*

(8.) What holiday does the heart symbolize?

Clue – *chocolates and flowers*

Answers to Fun Fact Questions:

(1.) The heart is located in the middle of the chest.

(2.) The size of your heart is approximately the same size as your fist.

(3.) The blue whale has the biggest heart.

(4.) The fruit fly has the smallest heart.

(5.) Of all the land animals, the giraffe has the largest heart.

(6.) The octopus has more than one heart. In fact, it has three hearts.

(7.) Doctors used to listen to the heart by pressing their ear against the patient's chest.

(8.) The heart symbolizes Valentine's Day, when we celebrate love.

Notes

_____

_____

_____

_____

_____

_____

_____

_____

_____

_____

Flip page to see interesting heart-related pictures.

World Heart Day

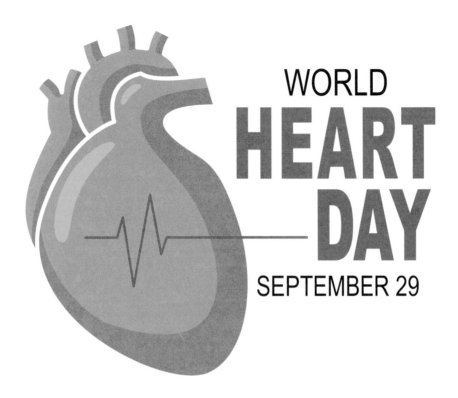

**WORLD
HEART
DAY**

SEPTEMBER 29

American Heart Month

American
Heart
Month

F E B R U A R Y

Human Heart

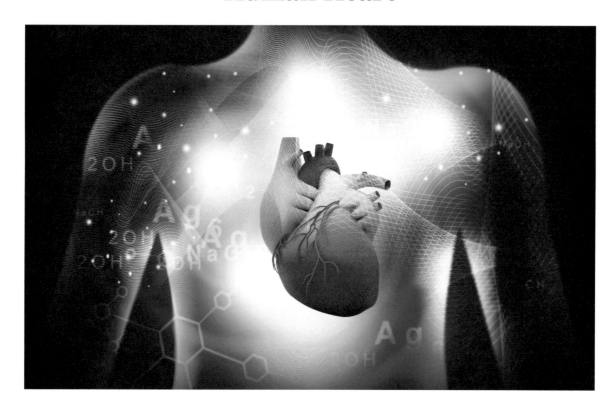

Our Heart

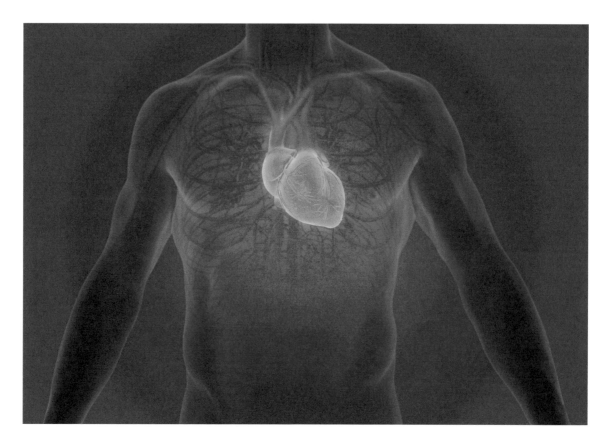

Heart with Lungs

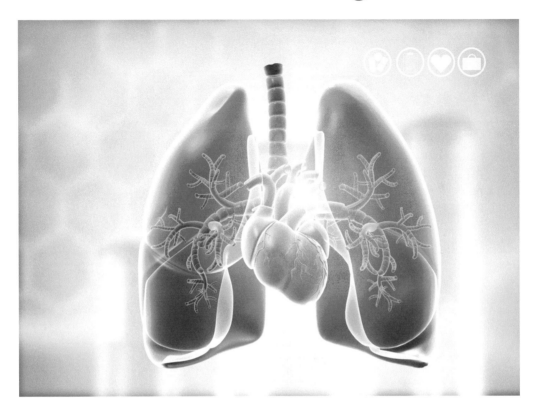

X-Ray

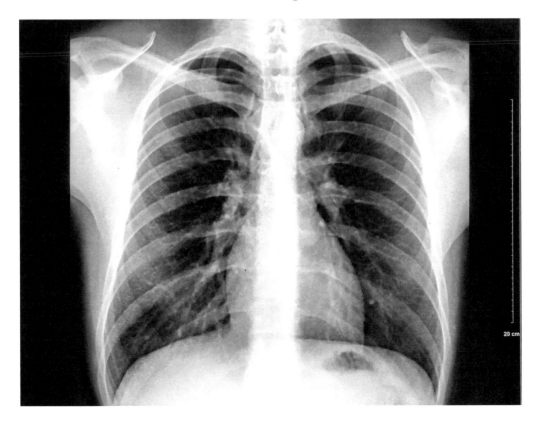

Blood Circulation

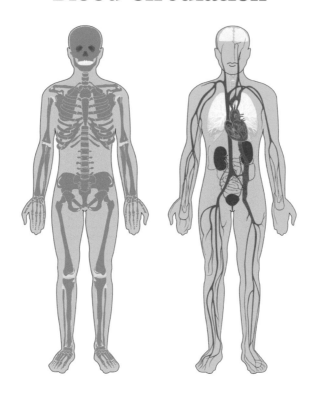

Inside of the Heart

Heart valve

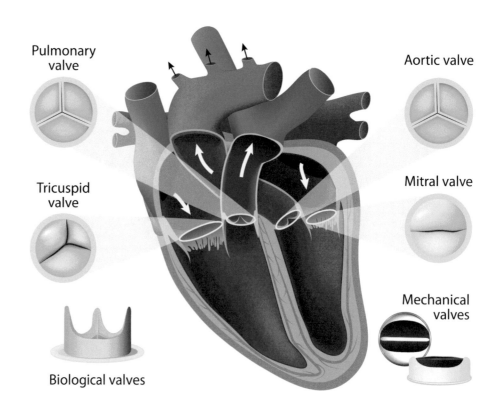

Pulmonary valve

Aortic valve

Tricuspid valve

Mitral valve

Biological valves

Mechanical valves

Dog Anatomy

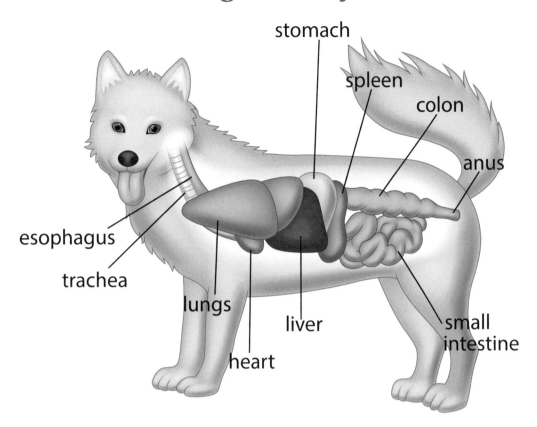

stomach

spleen

colon

anus

esophagus

trachea

lungs

heart

liver

small intestine

Cat Anatomy

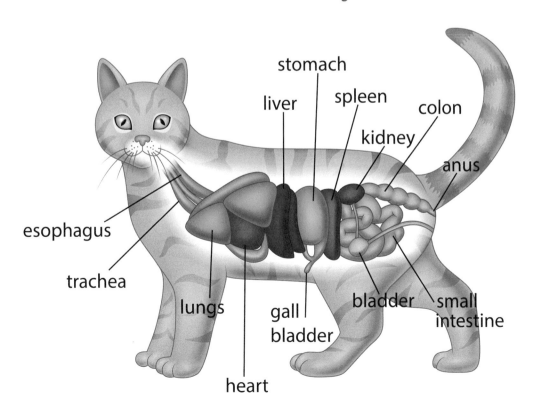

stomach

liver

spleen

colon

kidney

anus

esophagus

trachea

lungs

gall bladder

heart

bladder

small intestine

Vintage Stethoscope

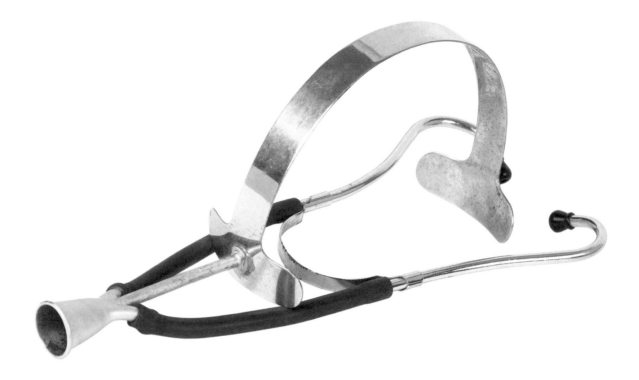

Wooden Stethoscope

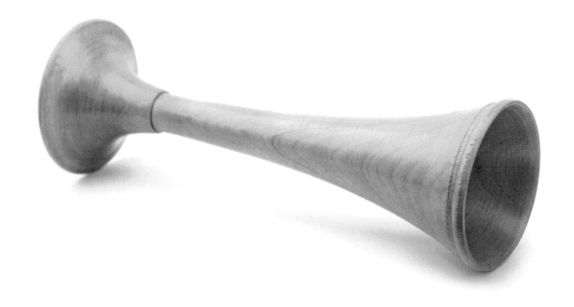

Vintage Medical Bag

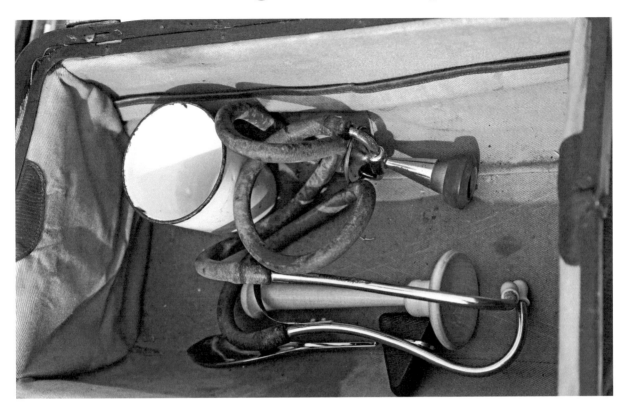

Vintage Doctor's Desk

Types of Heart Disease

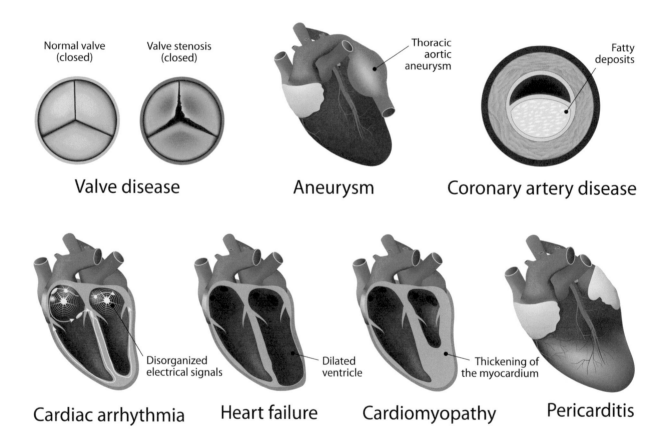

Normal valve (closed)   Valve stenosis (closed)

Valve disease

Thoracic aortic aneurysm

Aneurysm

Fatty deposits

Coronary artery disease

Disorganized electrical signals

Cardiac arrhythmia

Dilated ventricle

Heart failure

Thickening of the myocardium

Cardiomyopathy

Pericarditis

Heart Attack

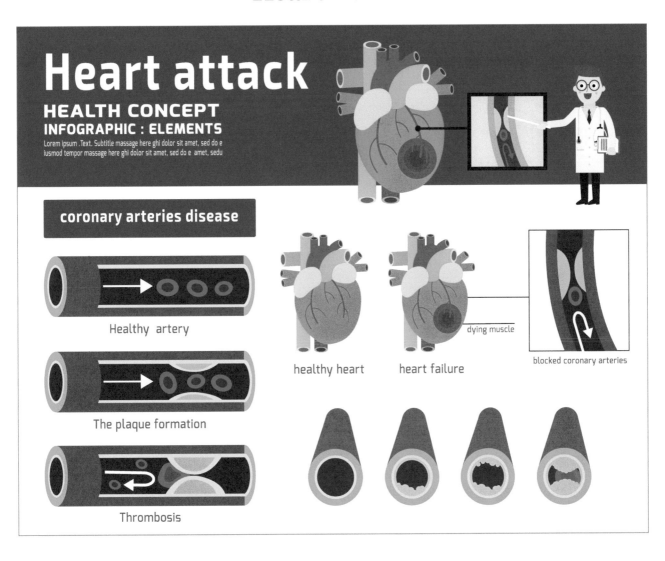

Heart attack

HEALTH CONCEPT
INFOGRAPHIC : ELEMENTS

Lorem ipsum .Text. Subtitle massage here ghi dolor sit amet, sed do e
iusmod tempor massage here ghi dolor sit amet, sed do e amet, sedu

coronary arteries disease

Healthy artery

The plaque formation

Thrombosis

healthy heart

heart failure

dying muscle

blocked coronary arteries

Bad Habits

SWEETS

JUNK FOOD

REST AT HOME

UNHEALTHY DRINKS

Good Habits

Bad Food

Good Food

Health Tips

EAT CLEAN

DRINK WATER

STAY ACTIVE

BE HEALTHY

Thanks to Our Heroes

Printed in the United States
by Baker & Taylor Publisher Services